P9-DUX-341

Praise for *One Blackbird at a Time*

Although these poems begin in the classroom, their reach feels limitless and wild. Here, seemingly anecdotal encounters with the work of Henry James, Virginia Woolf, or Robert Frost spiral into meditations on the lives of others, the complexities of our ethical decisions, the nuances of human relationships, and the certainties of mortality. It would be easy to say this is a book about teaching—it is!—but it's also a book about how our experience of reading humanizes us and shapes our experience of the world and other people. Wendy Barker's poems are rich, complex, and shimmering with energy and intelligence.

—Kevin Prufer, author of *In a Beautiful Country* and *Churches*

Wendy Barker's *One Blackbird at a Time* is a humorous and poignant meditation on what it is to be a professor of literature, what it could possibly mean in our era of visual literacy. *One Blackbird at a Time* makes a case for poetry—the poetry of the canon and the poetry of the now, i.e. Barker's own poetry. She takes on the big questions with smarts and a disarming joie de vivre. Her work is the best argument against "those who can't ___, teach." This is one can-do volume! Anyone who's ever been a student will want to read *One Blackbird at a Time* to find out what it is like on the other side of the desk.

—Denise Duhamel, author of *Blowout* and *Ka-Ching!*

Like a favorite class, the whole of *One Blackbird at a Time* is greater than the sum of its parts, although the individual poems stand up exquisitely well on their own. Decades of teachers and students will see themselves in these poems.

—David Dooley, *Paterson Literary Review*

The poems begin depicting classroom discussions of literature—largely the standards of introductory surveys—then deftly pivot to smart, ranging meditations on contemporary culture, family connection, and loss . . . . And one needn't be an educator to delight in Barker's generous humanist vision.

—Benjamin S. Grossberg, *Antioch Review*

Wendy Barker's keen eye for detail results in one of the most exciting and original poetry collections I have read for a long time.

—Valerie Morton, *Galatea Resurrects*

One *Blackbird* at a Time

Other Books by Wendy Barker

POETRY

Books

Nothing Between Us: The Berkeley Years
Poems from Paradise
Way of Whiteness
Let the Ice Speak
Winter Chickens and Other Poems

Chapbooks

Things of the Weather
Between Frames
Eve Remembers

Translations

Tagore: Final Poems (with Saranindranath Tagore)

PROSE

Poems' Progress
The House Is Made of Poetry: The Art of Ruth Stone, co-edited with Sandra M. Gilbert
Lunacy of Light: Emily Dickinson and the Experience of Metaphor

One *Blackbird* at a Time

Wendy Barker

Winner of the John Ciardi Prize for Poetry
Selected by Alice Friman

BkMk Press
University of Missouri-Kansas City

Copyright © 2015 by Wendy Barker

BkMk Press
University of Missouri-Kansas City
5101 Rockhill Road
Kansas City, MO 64110
www.umkc.edu/bkmk

Financial assistance for this project has been provided by
the Missouri Arts Council, a state agency.

Executive Editor: Robert Stewart
Managing Editor: Ben Furnish
Associate Editor: Michelle Boisseau
Assistant Managing Editor: Cynthia Beard
Cover art: Michael Mayhugh

BkMk Press wishes to thank Marie Mayhugh, Cameron Morse,
Anders Carlson, Brittany Green.

The John Ciardi Prize for Poetry thanks Walter Bargen, Greg Field, Lindsey Martin-Bowen,
Linda Rodriguez, Maryfrances Wagner.

Library of Congress Cataloging-in-Publication Data

Barker, Wendy.
[Poems. Selections]
One blackbird at a time / Wendy Barker.
pages ; cm
"Winner of the John Ciardi Prize for Poetry selected by Alice Friman."
ISBN 978-1-943491-03-2 (acid-free paper)
I. Title.
PS3552.A67124A6 2015
811'.54--dc23
2015036459

ISBN 978-1-943491-03-2

This book is set in Garamond and Gill Sans.

Acknowledgments

I am grateful to the editors of the following magazines, in which some of these poems first appeared, at times in slightly different versions.

Barn Owl Review	"Whenever We've Dipped into *Walden*"
Cerise Press	"In the Seminar, Trying to Launch *Passage to India*" and "Waking Over *Call It Sleep*"
Connecticut Review	"Arriving at Wallace Stevens in the 13th Week" and "Emily in the Classroom"
Crab Creek Review	"After Spring Break, Arriving at Pound's 'In a Station of the Metro,'" "Alone in the Museum's Greek Collection," and "Coming to Cather"
Diode	"Langston Hughes' 'Weary Blues'" and "His Eyelashes Are Not Tarantulas"
Gettysburg Review	"On Teaching Too Many Victorian Novels in Too Short a Space of Time During Which I Become"
Lips	"I'd Said It Would Be"
Matter Press	"Wang Wei in the Workshop"
Mid-American Review	"Why I Dread Teaching *The Sun Also Rises*" and "In Our Class on Roethke"
New Letters	"I'm Not Sure the Cherry Is the 'Loveliest of Trees'"
Paterson Literary Review	"About That 'One Art,'" "Innisfree, They Get," and "Next-to-Last Week in the Senior Workshop"
Southern Review	"I Hate Telling People I Teach English," "Teaching 'The Red Wheelbarrow' the 30th Time," "Teaching *Mrs. Dalloway* I'm Thinking," "The Last Time I Taught Robert Frost," "Truth, Beauty, and the Intro Poetry Workshop," "Books, Bath Towels, and Beyond," "Rereading *The Golden Bowl*," "Ending the Semester in American Lit," and "The Morning After Our Second Ecopoetry Class"
Water~Stone Review	"Preparing Jeffers 'Vulture' Before Class"

"Books, Bath Towels, and Beyond" is included in *The Best American Poetry 2013*, eds. Denise Duhamel and David Lehman (Scribner). "Teaching *Mrs. Dalloway* I'm Thinking" and "Teaching 'The Red Wheelbarrow' the 30th Time" were reprinted on VerseDaily, www.versedaily.org. "Teaching 'The Red Wheelbarrow' the 30th Time," "Innisfree, They Get," "Langston Hughes' 'Weary Blues,'" and "In Our Class on Roethke" are all included in *Poets on Growth*, eds. Peter LaBerge and Talin Tahajian (Math Paper). "Why I Dread Teaching *The Sun Also Rises*" was reprinted in *Women Write Resistance: Poets Resist Gender Violence*, ed. Laura Madeline Wiseman (Hyacinth Girl). "Ending the Semester in American Lit" is included in *Raising Lilly Ledbetter: Women Poets Occupy the Workspace*, eds. Carolyne Wright, M. L. Lyons, and Eugenia Toledo (Lost Horse Press).

I owe reams of thanks to the generous friends who provided help with a number of these poems: Kacee Belcher, Ralph Black, Chana Bloch, David Dooley, Sandra M. Gilbert, Jeannine Keenan, Alicia Ostriker, and David Ray Vance. Denise Duhamel, Catherine Kasper, and Barbara Ras made excellent suggestions for the manuscript. And I owe much to the University of Texas at San Antonio for institutional support, especially Bernadette Andrea, Mark Bayer, Bridget Drinka, and Daniel J. Gelo. I'm extremely grateful to Alice Friman, and to Michelle Boisseau and Ben Furnish of BkMk Press for such excellent care and advice. And without Jacqueline Kolosov and my two Bolinas Salon compadres, Kevin Clark and Hannah Stein, who spent more time with these poems than they should have, this entire collection could never have taken shape. I must also offer heartfelt thanks to my son, David Barker, and my sisters, Trisha McConnell and Liza Piatt, for their understanding, support, and encouragement. And finally, I want to express immeasurable gratitude to my husband Steven G. Kellman, who read and reread drafts upon drafts of these poems and whose quiet, dependable rhythms make dailiness a poem.

Contents

Foreword by Alice Friman *13*

I
I Hate Telling People I Teach English 17

II
Truth, Beauty, and the Intro Poetry Workshop 21
Emily in the Classroom 23
His Eyelashes Are Not Tarantulas 24
Waking Over *Call It Sleep* 26
I'd Said It Would Be 29
In the Seminar, Trying to Launch *Passage to India* 31

III
About That "One Art" 37
Teaching *Mrs. Dalloway* I'm Thinking 38
Alone in the Museum's Greek Collection 39
On Teaching Too Many Victorian Novels in Too Short
a Space of Time During Which I Become 40
Rereading *The Golden Bowl* 41
Wang Wei in the Workshop 43
Langston Hughes' "Weary Blues" 44
Why I Dread Teaching *The Sun Also Rises* 45

IV
Whenever We've Dipped into *Walden* 51
Preparing Jeffers' "Vulture" Before Class 53
Innisfree, They Get 55
I'm Not Sure the Cherry Is the "Loveliest of Trees" 56
Coming to Cather 58
The Morning After Our Second Ecopoetry Class 60

V
Teaching "The Red Wheelbarrow" the 30th Time 65
After Spring Break, Arriving at Pound's "In a Station of the Metro" 67
Arriving at Wallace Stevens in the 13th Week 69
Next-to-Last Week in the Senior Workshop 70
Books, Bath Towels, and Beyond 71
In Our Class on Roethke 73
Ending the Semester in American Lit 75
The Last Time I Taught Robert Frost 77

Foreword

Wendy Barker's *One Blackbird at a Time* is not a how-to book, an instruction manual about teaching literature in today's college classroom, although there's many a valuable tip one can learn here. Nor is the book a sort of memoir in verse, a this-is-what-happened-to-me book, although it's all there—the struggle, the necessary patience, the frustration, the successes. No, this collection is an unabashed love letter, a love letter to literature and the power of art. Generous and inclusive, Barker opens up her classroom, pushes back the walls, to reach out to anyone who ever opened a book, who trembled by the tracks with Anna Karenina; who understands, in some hiding place in the brain, Frost's "dark and deep" and the stopgap rationalization of "miles to go before I sleep." What Barker shows in these finely crafted and honest poems is what literature still has the power to do despite sound bites, commercials, political spin, and all the distortions of language we live with. At base, reading down through layers of Barker's insight, remembrance, and even confession, these poems and the literature they examine affect everyone. In this classroom, no one is exempt. Not the students, not the reader, and—bless her—not the teacher.

—Alice Friman

I Hate Telling People I Teach English

Like last August, after they'd finished my bone scan,
this combed-over mid-sixties guy starts chatting about the novel
he's written in his head, he only needs someone like me
to work it up, he never liked punctuation, parts of speech, all that junk
from junior high, and I couldn't get my print-out fast enough
to take to my GP, who likes to quote from his inspirational speeches
to local luncheon clubs. He's determined to collect them
in a book, though he'd need a good editor, do I know any, and meanwhile
I've been waiting fifty-seven minutes for help with recharging
my sluggish thyroid, and I haven't met any doctors who like giving
free advice about your daughter's milk allergy or your friend's
migraines or the thumb you slammed in the stairwell door, splitting it
open so badly your students interrupted your lecture on
pronoun agreement to note you were dripping blood from your hand
and wow, what happened? But it's mostly at parties I hate
admitting I teach English. I've never been quick enough to fudge,
the way a Methodist minister friend says he's in "support
services" so he doesn't get called to lead grace. I guess I could dub myself
a "communications facilitator," but since I'm in the business
of trying to obviate obfuscation, I own up, though I dread what I know
is coming: "Oh," they say, "I hated English, all that grammar,
you won't like the way I talk, you'll be correcting me," and suddenly
they need another Bud or merlot or they've got to check out
the meatballs or guacamole over on the table and I'm left facing
blank space, no one who can even think about correcting
my dangling participles. Once when the computer guy was at the house,
bent over my laptop trying to get us back online,
he asked what it was I wrote, and when I told him "poetry," said, "Ah—
fluffy stuff," and I wasn't sure whether he was kidding
or not, but I figured at least it was better than his saying he hated poetry
or that he had a manuscript right outside in his Camry and
could I take a look, no hurry, but he knew it would sell, could I tell him
how to get an agent for his novel about his uncle
moving to Arizona and running a thriving ostrich farm until the day
hot-air balloons took off a half mile away

and stampeded the birds, till all he was left with were feathers and bloody tangled necks on fence posts, the dream of making two million

from those birds a haunting sentence fragment—but then, I think: I would never have wanted to miss the time a dentist,

tapping my molars, asked if I'd like to hear him recite Chaucer's Prologue to *The Canterbury Tales* in Middle English, which he did

while I lay back in his chair, open-mouthed, pierced to the root.

Truth, Beauty, and the Intro Poetry Workshop

Still prickling from a neighbor's yelling "Shove it
up your ass" when all I'd done was ask if
he could stop his terriers
from yapping all night, I wasn't entirely patient when
the kid with the scarab tattoos effused about
beauty, said ever since Brit Lit
he's wanted to talk like Milton—"Yet once more, O ye
Laurels"—or Keats—"Those lips, O slippery
blisses, twinkling eyes," adding
he's in the class to "build the lofty rhyme." I reminded him
it's 2010, we don't wear cravats or corsets and
nobody waltzes anymore. He nodded,
so I asked what music he likes. "Deathcore—It Dies Today
and Suicide Silence," he said, and then,
"I'm a drummer." "Aha," I said,
"how about writing a poem the way you wield those sticks." Now
he's turned in a free-verse sequence leaded
with expletives about arguments
with his crack-dealing brother who never leaves the house without
his .38. His lines reverberate with the turbulence
of a 747 out of LAX. Yet I'm
lashing myself, worrying I did him wrong. I love Auden's
call to "Let the healing fountain start" from
"the deserts of the heart,"
but why not water this kid's land-mine-loaded sand
dunes with a little harmony? The human soul
needs beauty more
than bread, said Lawrence. Haven't I been yearning for a bit
of old-school beauty myself? Just last week
we watched a tennis princess
swear she'd take her fuckin' ball and slam it down the fuckin'
judge's throat. I know poetry's got to breathe
with the fumes of its time,

but I'd like to escape my own, forget about drugged-up
kids with guns. And it isn't even true nobody
waltzes anymore. How
could I have forgotten that night downtown a year ago
when, as the symphony in the outdoor pavilion
lilted into "The Blue Danube,"
a thousand people all joined in, arms lifting to arms,
lovers and uncles, grandmas and bikers, moms
and toddlers dancing
under the moon to soaring melodies barely heard these days,
till we became one rhapsodic, dactylic swirl.

Emily in the Classroom

Hovers at the ceiling's buzzing
fluorescent lights. The students crack
their paperbacks, pressing
the valves of her phrases, working them
like bellows, determined
to ignite a fire with compacted air, evade
the cold that could razor the tops
of our heads. They want to illuminate
the shadowy dashes, the slivered
chasms, seal them for safe-keeping
under glass. She hovers
at the ceiling like an unfamiliar freckled
moth, like Jehovah—Yahweh—
a name we cannot speak aloud. She is
hovering like a breath taken
further and further until released,
a slip of thread lifted
by the wind. If only they could spread
their feathers, gain an arc,
know how neighborly, the invisible.

His Eyelashes Are Not Tarantulas

But I've been bitten, stung, and I want to tell this guy, star pitcher
on the university team—bare
arms so muscular I'm amazed
any straight woman around this table can utter a word—I'd like to shred
his printout and toss the pieces into
the nearest recycle bin. His poem
begins with a guy who's salivating for a "she" who's lolling her curves
on his kitchen counter, but when the "I"
licks and nibbles "her" moist flesh,
we learn "she" is only an apple. How do I count the ways I could sneer
his poem's fouled out? The students
are chuckling, "great humor," Adrian's
saying, but I'm struggling to calm down, behave like the mature workshop
leader I'm supposed to be while my mind
races like a runner stealing
third. I'm hurled back fifty-some years to my first steady boyfriend,
the one I even thought about marrying,
record-breaking pitcher on
our high school team, black lashes, eyes dark as Medjool dates. This kid
looks just like that boy. Something very sexy
about a pitcher—I'd sit behind
home plate—the ball coming right at me after the long wind up, intense
crouch over the mound. He made it
to the majors, the Braves, and once
I saw him pitch against Willie McCovey. I'd love to watch my student
in action. I saw the old boyfriend last
summer, after all these years, and
over lunch, without a smile, he reminded me I'd dumped him not once
but twice. He'd never forgiven me, his back
rigid as a Louisville Slugger while
he insisted on paying the bill. Or was he bored and eager to leave? When
was it students began to see me as old enough
to be their mother? That September

afternoon Marissa said in my office, "Oh Dr. Barker, your shoes are
adorable, they're just like the ones my mom
wears!" Now the apple arcs from
another direction—Belinda says maybe the poem's about sadness over
a woman's desertion, so all the man's left with
is one apple on the countertop. But—
I'll admit it—though this kid could be my grandson, he's so damned cute
I'm smitten and all too aware I've been
dropped from the team. Where is
that smooth-skinned girl my boyfriend loved? Forget the snide remarks
I'd wanted to make, the rant about
Rossetti's *Goblin Market* with
those leering men offering fruit so tongue-luscious you grew addicted,
sickened, died. Forget my desire to snipe
that women are not grapes, plums
waiting for hornets, yellow jackets, to sting them dry. So I tell him
to read Shakespeare, write a new poem
showing a lover as nothing like
a piece of fruit—and add that he'd throw a three-pitch strike-out
if he just described an apple
so we'd hanker for its tang.

Waking Over *Call It Sleep*

I'm the closest thing to Jewish in the class even though
at best I'm only one-eighth, according
to my English mother, who insisted the shadowy figure
of her granny was a Jew since nobody knew
her origins and everybody talked as if something had been
hushed up, shameful, and of course
everything about her hawk-nosed face was unusually dark,
especially the ringlets of her unruly hair,
or I suppose you could count the fact that I'm married
to a man whose grandparents arrived
at Ellis Island from what is now Ukraine only three years
after Henry Roth, yet none of these
students has the *seykhl* to know their teacher is a *shiksa*
and our group is as goyish as pork chops
but they've all been children, and they love this novel,
they know what it's like to be
speechless, powerless, afraid. Nobody needs me to explain
the terror of what lies beyond
the front door and what lies within, and the paralysis
that comes from never knowing
when to dash outside or stand by the window behind
the blinds. One year, while we were reading
Ginsberg, I knew I'd have to describe Kaddish
though I'd never even heard it
recited, but I gave it a go, saying in passing that only
1% of our city's population is Jewish
which was when Heather quipped: "Of course, they're all
in Hollywood making millions from
trashy movies." I put down my book and didn't move—
you could hear the whirr
of the elevator down the hall. When I spoke, I said, "That
was a very offensive comment"—and
I realized I was shaking, after decades of holding forth
in linoleum-floored classrooms. It wasn't
like the times I've heard someone saying *wet* meaning

wetback which are both despicable
terms and I argue those too, but this time it was as if
I'd been slapped full in the face, called
sheeny, kike, and I swear that tears came to my eyes though
I couldn't cry out "*Gevalt*, help,
take that back, you ignorant little bitch." The tension lasted
beyond the ten-minute break, which
I loosened to twenty, and not just for the smokers. Now
I've handed out maps that highlight
Galicia, Brooklyn, Tysmenicz, the Lower East Side,
Avenue D, and 9th Street, and a list with
explanations of terms: Passover, Ashkenazi, knish, shul,
and pogrom. We talk about Friday night
and the candles, and everyone is right there in the room
with Roth and with me and with my husband
who joins us after the break to tell about the author's
life with his duck farm and his goyish wife
and his writer's block, and I begin to wonder if any of these
students with family from Monterrey or
Laredo will some day learn—as a friend of mine did last year—
that a great-great-great-and-beyond
grandfather came over from Spain to escape the Inquisition,
and if it will happen—as my friend Raul
told me it did—that in the lighting of candles with relatives
gathered for a first Shabbat, an elderly aunt
in the corner will begin to sigh and to weep, and when they
press her, ask her what's wrong,
she'll tell them she's suddenly remembering an abuela
who covered her face with her hands
every Friday night to greet the Divine, the Shekhinah,
and who every week sent one grandchild
to buy candles. A child, I'm thinking, who wore a silver
cross around her neck and had never
heard *judía de mierda* hurled in her face with the auto-pilot
contempt of the six girls who chanted

at me in the bathroom once during second grade, as they
pointed at the color of my striped
dress: "Blue, blue, you're a Jew," but I didn't get it—
I thought they were saying *jewel.*

I'd Said It Would Be

Depressing, and in fact I dreaded it, hadn't even requested it,
an entire course on 19th Century literature by women. We'll feel
corseted, starved for breath, I warned on the first day,
and sure enough, after *Jane Eyre, Goblin Market, Uncle Tom's Cabin*,
and *Incidents in the Life of a Slave Girl*, when we come to Alcott's
Little Women, the whole class sighs in relief to read about Jo,
loping like an unfettered colt down the road, chomping apples
in the attic with a rat. Claudia says she liked the way Winona Rider
wore Converse high-tops to create an authentic
athletic bounce in the film with Susan Sarandon who—everyone
agrees—was not our idea of Marmee, the mother we all wish had been
ours, who never lost it, never flew off the handle
and screamed at a daughter for spilling a glass of milk. But then
Holly reminds us that Marmee confessed to Jo she'd been angry
every single day of her life. She'd kept it inside,
pushed it in, just as those corsets pressed hard on a woman's ribs,
constricted the lungs, the intestines. Liveliest discussion of the whole
semester. Though am I the only one who never
identified with Jo, but with Meg, fretting about clothes? All this
week I've been poring over catalogs, pondering whether I could risk
one of those gauzy, swirly skirts everybody's wearing now. Yesterday,
shopping for new bras, I grew dizzy wandering through racks
of styles and almost all of them gel-filled or molded so that,
trying them on, I felt like two Wagnerian breastplates
had been glued to my chest, and I couldn't get out of there
fast enough, once again lamenting the passing of the '60s, when
we happily flopped around under our blouses, free
at last. How is it, then, that while every woman in this room
proclaims her sisterhood with Jo, I'm facing a barrage of breasts
bulging from lacey camisoles and push-up bras in this
roomful of moussed, streaked and unstreaked, upswept and
downswept spiral-curled locks of hair? Here we are, in
the twenty-first century, and we're still obsessing,

jittery, even frantic about judgments from the telescopic
lenses of the world beyond our closet door. The Academy
Awards focus less on the arts of acting and
cinematography than on Penelope Cruz's "white embellished
strapless gown" with its "luscious satin folds." I won't ask
how long Claudia takes to do her hair so it lifts a hillock
over her head and then drops like a waterfall, an auburn-
streaked cascade. As long, I'd think, as it took to arrange
Marianne Dashwood's looped-up ringlets in *Sense*
and Sensibility. I know the '90s ushered in the era of Girl Power,
and I'm not the sort of second-wave feminist who'll be
buried in her Birkenstocks, but I doubt we've made
that much progress when our guys slouch around all comfy
in tee-shirts and baggy jeans. I guess one of those swirly skirts
might look okay on me, as long as I wore opaque
stockings, hid my varicose shins. How I wish we could break
out of this whale-boned century and move on, at least
to the twentieth. Fast forward to Harjo, gallop
like horses of "fur and teeth," horses that burn like stars. Strip
down to hard, unadorned muscle and flesh, wade into Lucille
Clifton's poems, shake ungirdled hips with "space
to move around in." But we're laced tight to the syllabus, and
the only way out is for Jane Eyre to marry her Rochester,
for Jo March to wed Professor Bhaer, her "bear,"
after learning to bite her "abominable tongue." How long
before someone, anyone in this room, will begin to growl?

In the Seminar, Trying to Launch *Passage to India*

I've got to lecture on Forster and the Raj, the partition of Bengal,
but I can't focus, and it's not only
that I'm remembering my own months
in India, the smells of cardamom, turmeric mingling with charcoal
smoke amid rickshaws, water
buffalo, bicycles, camels, and eighteen
wheelers. It's that I'm still twitchy about the Englishness I inherited
from my mother, who sailed
to New York from Southampton
on the Queen Mary. So when Lisa complains the novel is confusing,
she can't keep track of the weird
names, I push my notes aside. "Okay,"
I say, "Let's make a list, start with the Brits." "Hopeless," spouts Richard,
"they're racists, all of them, imperialist
capitalists using their hegemonic power
to oppress the indigenous people. Detestable, disgusting, especially
Miss Quested," he grumbles. I've been
dealing with my Anglophobia
for years, ashamed of the way my mother and her snobbish brother
would blithely butcher names
of places, saying "Urnuhk*oo*lum"
instead of "Ern*ä*kulam," with the emphasis on the wrong syllable. But
before I can ask if everyone in the class
found *all* the Brits in the novel
despicable, Lupita asks why they have to live off by themselves
on the hill. "Because they like
playing royalty," sneers Richard,
adding, "They're recreating their own little England with their canned
peas and their stupid plays." He's
right. Yet I can't forget my third day
in Delhi, when Manjit led me into the sudden calm of the Hyatt
and fed me a lemon lassi, saying
she could see I'd been about to
go under from too much India too fast. And I'd thought myself
the consummate traveler—a dozen

stamps on my passport. I won't
mention the time on the beach south of Chennai when a horde
of kids followed me, clutching
at my kameez till I broke free
and stumbled into an Anglican church with its pews lined up
in rows. If it had been
1920, with a pink-cheeked British
officer nearby, I could have blubbered about those hateful boys
taunting and poking, could have
created as big a crisis as Adela Quested
when she accuses Aziz of accosting her in the cave. Now Marcy
is asking what the British were
doing in India anyway, and I've
got to backtrack to Elizabeth I, tea, opium, and indigo. But I hear
the fluting voice of my English
granny, a governess in the Punjab
who regretted the return to London, where she missed the neem
trees, the banyans, the spices,
the Bhatnagar family, and the bulbul's
song. "So what happened in the Malabar Caves," Annie is asking,
and Cathy answers: "Before Adela
entered the cavern, she was
Ronny Heaslop's fiancée, but inside the cave, she heard the voice
of her real self, so when she
came out, she'd changed,
just like India changed him, he's not the same guy she knew
in England, he's turned into
a bureaucratic jerk." And Michael
adds that, "After Adela left the cave, she heard an echo in her ear till
she finally confesses Aziz had
never bothered her at all." I didn't
know, when I arrived at JFK's Gate B31 for my first flight to Delhi,
my eyes the only blue ones among
hundreds slouched in plastic

chairs, waiting to board, that when I returned home I'd be headed
for a divorce. And I didn't
know, in towns like Ludhiana,
some men knew American women only from TV, believed us
all to be sluts, so I was half
embarrassed and half flattered
at the dinner party where the guy kept snuggling up, calling me
Marilyn Monroe, me with my
breasts no bigger than dollops of dal,
with my gray-blond hair, while my horrified elegant hosts
pried him away. But now
I'm telling the students how
I learned to say "atcha" in Punjabi, the one word I was sure I could
master, trying over and over until,
furious at my inability even to pronounce
the word for "okay," I lost it, blew up, hissed, snorted "uh-*chah*"
as loud as I could, and the whole
room shouted, I'd done it, I'd gotten it,
I could almost pass for Punjabi. Now even Richard is laughing. Yet
I don't mention how angry
I really was, how exhausted, frustrated,
and, unlike Adela Quested, up to my neck in "the real India,"
even though people were
oh, so kind, exclaiming how well
I was managing for my first time. The fluorescent lights begin
their erratic, crackling hum,
and Lisa catches my eye,
plunges in: "Mrs. Moore got it, didn't she, she liked sitting with Aziz
in the temple, he even
praised her by saying she was
'Oriental,' but why did she freak out in the caves?" Cathy explains
that "Mrs. Moore had trusted
people's goodness, but
inside the cave, all her old beliefs are erased. And see how on page 223
Forster says Mrs. Moore wasn't

the 'dear old lady' everyone
thought, India 'brought her into the open.'" Michael, José, and
Annie are nodding. Marcy is
jotting notes. I give it a minute,
take a long breath. "You know," I say, "we're all tired. What if
we quit for now. I'll see you
next week." But before I let them go—
I can't stop myself—I tell them about the first night I ever spent
in India, when the lock
to my room at the Delhi
YWCA wouldn't open from the inside, and my friends kept calling,
but the phone didn't work
and I couldn't figure out
how to let them know I was trapped until the clerk at the desk
agreed to break the rules
and allow my frantic
university hosts to climb the stairs and bang on my door, holler
at me, "*Are you there? Are you there?*"
like a blinding echo, and
I wasn't even sure if I was, or when I got out, who I would be.

About That "One Art"

It's a perfect poem, I say, and though no one
in the class is over twenty-five, everybody
nods. They've all lost: the Madame
Alexander doll fallen into the toilet, silky
hair never the same, the friend who
moved away to Dallas, a brother once again
in juvie. So many schools—thirteen in
a dozen years—I lost each friend I made
till grad school. And every move since,
something always missing—this last time,
the box that held my photo albums
of the sixties, that elastic, unveined life I'd
love to visit just once more. And now
the husbands of so many have diminished—
the cancerous prostates, the double
bypasses, the radiation, the chemo. One died
while napping. And how many women friends
have lost a breast? Or two? Now I wonder,
who'll be leaving first: me, or you? Just how
will that be mastered? And how is it even time
begins to lose itself? In class I ask why Bishop
wrote the poem as a villanelle, and so we
parse the form, say how such echoing
slows us, keeps us focused on each single
disappearance, so at first we hear lightheartedness,
a witty irony—but then the sounds grow
vaster, catch us off guard. And quicken.

Teaching *Mrs. Dalloway* I'm Thinking

How I'd like to buy flowers, how I'd like to place a sterling
silver bowl of peonies or cut-glass vase of tulips and irises
on the laminate seminar table in this windowless room,
and I'm thinking how I'd like to arrive before the one student
always a half-hour early, how I'd like to greet each of them
at the door, inquire after their sisters and cousins, their tíos
and abuelitas, and comfort the one who's been fired
from his job. Every Tuesday another novel about the modern
condition, those catchy phrases we use: "alienation
and fragmentation"—while for the past three weeks Jill,
the debate team captain on two scholarships, hasn't said
a word because, she told me sobbing at the break, her boyfriend
was found bloody in his apartment, shot by her brother
off his meds, and Angie, dispatching for Pleasure U Hot Line,
her shift moved to graveyard, slumps dozing
in her chair. Now Jeffrey is saying, "She's snobbish, Clarissa,
I don't like her, who cares about her maids and
her flowers, but she's right, I mean, she gets it, nothing like
a great party." It's the dinner hour, though no bells chime
on this campus, and only two of us have actually heard Big Ben,
have ever strolled through Regent's Park, ridden on
a red double-decker. But nobody around this table wonders
why Septimus hurls himself out the window, nobody
needs PTSD explained, and when Marita asks, "Wasn't it Woolf
who filled her pockets with stones and walked into
a river?" nobody says "weird," their two dozen heads bent over
pages littered with post-its. I'm thinking how I want
to say something, mend this rent in the air the way Clarissa
gathers the raveled threads of her ripped dress with a needle,
the way she draws everyone into her party, but already it's time
to pack up our pens, our notebooks, head out on the crowded
interstate, past all the newly constructed buildings with no
balconies, no wrought iron railings, these multiple stories
of steel and glass, mirrored so no one can see into them.

Alone In the Museum's Greek Collection

Of course I'm reminded of "Ode on a Grecian
Urn," and wonder if, next fall when I teach Keats again,
I could bring the class to peer through all this glass
at the dozens of amphorae on their crisp laminate
stands. Amphora: from the Greek "to bear." And
how these urns bear up, carry sketches of a life we can
barely conjure, the pregnant middles of these glossy
vessels displaying such slender, muscular boys, heroes,
goddesses—and the Furies. But I fear I'd ignore
the students—I'd be mesmerized—as I am now—by an urn
labeled "Attic Red-Figure Column-Krater." Here's Orestes
kneeling on a pile of rocks, head bowed to the winged
Fury on his left, snakes writhing round
her arms. He's just killed his mother and her lover,
revenge for their slaying his father. His body is contorted,
knees and feet turned toward Apollo and Artemis, who
stand opposite, as if to offer solace. He seems
almost ripped in half. The way judges might absolve us,
saying "rightful cause," or a minister, reminding us we're
only human, and yet we're chased for years, threatened
with all the Furies' snakes. I think of the words
I muttered in the doorway of the room where
my mother lay dying, hurtful words she may have heard,
and of the words I couldn't say during the days before
my father died. There was the time I shook
and shook my colicky infant son and screamed
into his tiny face when he'd been crying for hours
and nothing I'd done could soothe him—his shrieks
shifted then to terror. Those Furies still
know where to find me, hurling their hissing vipers
around my shoulders. Though Aeschylus tells us Orestes
will be absolved, there's no release shown on this jar,
his body twisting at the core. Families—
the wars within that shape the wars without. How
can our deeds be laid to rest? Ripples in perpetuity.

On Teaching Too Many Victorian Novels in Too Short a Space of Time During Which I Become

Stuffed, like a twenty-pound turkey crammed to the crust-slithery maw
not with croutons and giblets, but ribbons, pendants, waistcoats, ruffles, and plumes
till I'm dazed, logy, needing a nap trying to keep track during eight hundred
pages of Bulstrodes, Cadwalladers, Featherstones, Chicheleys, Plymdales, Hackbutts,
and Minchins, when those English villages didn't hold as many people as I pass
on the interstate in fifteen minutes or dodge at the mall the day after Thanksgiving
or slump down with at the gate waiting for the delayed flight or stare at on CNN
or MSNBC in an hour, surfing through head after talking head, each expounding
to me lounging on my couch as though we were all seated around a mahogany table
loaded with glistening plate and leaded goblets, embossed napkins, and candelabras.
But the sixteen of us at five metal-legged tables jigsawed together in our department's
closet of a seminar room, with no possibility of pushing back chairs, leaning into pillows,
gazing into a fire, and holding to the light a snifter of cognac the color of autumn
leaves somewhere in an English village, are chatting away as though we are neighbors,
as if the characters in *Middlemarch* lived next door, and we've become vicar, solicitor,
seamstress, and a cousin all rolled into one, as we analyze Dorothea's encumbered vistas,
Lydgate's tightening financial noose—how lonely, how restricted, we say, grateful
for the roominess, the promise of our lives, though none of us mentions our MasterCard
or Chevy Avalanche payments, just as we ignore the fact that few of us have met
our own neighbors, since nobody ever asks anybody over for tea or drinks or Scrabble,
and if somebody is burgled or shot, we might hear about it on the car radio
driving home after Monday's six o'clock class, another night without dinner.

Rereading *The Golden Bowl*

I'd rather carry my grandmother's iridescent
Tiffany vase across six rutted parking lots while rolling
my briefcase and gripping my lunch than teach this
book. When it comes to the Master, I want to keep him
to myself, thread my own way through
polished drawing rooms and twisting garden paths. I'd
rather feel that if I'm hanging fire, speechless
in the middle of class, musing over Maggie's ruminations
to Fanny—all those suspicions about her
husband and her father's wife—I can pause as long as
I'd like. When Grandma's vase crashed
from the table, I was never sure whether the neighbor's
elbow had jostled it or my German shepherd's
tail. Two months after I'd rescued it from my cousin's
garage sale, potter friends explained
what the etched *L.C.T.* on the bottom meant, and then,
the next day, it shattered. We live our
lives through objects, I've heard an artist say. I glued
the fragments, a crude joining, but
the best I could do. All the flaws, visible and invisible,
within marriages. Friends of a woman I love
keep urging her to dump her imperious husband of forty
years. But once, when I dropped her off after
a Woody Allen film, before I pulled out of the drive,
I saw her through the front door's oval glass
with that potbellied man, an embrace so tender, so rapt,
I wanted to stay right there in my car in the dark,
absorb some of that closeness. How do we ever know
what goes on between any couple? Why
people stay, or wriggle free, or bolt? Maggie's husband
seems every inch a prince, though we begin
to wonder. Then we question our wondering. I'm finally
having Grandma's vase restored, by a woman
who understands glass. She says when she's finished
we'll barely see the gaps missing their

minuscule shards. Favrile—its color shifts as you turn it in the light, violet to green to blue and
rose. A technique Tiffany patented in 1894, ten years before the novel. It's not that
Maggie really lied, but that her subtle phrasings mended her marriage—in the end, everyone was
"magnificent." For Henry James, broadcasting naked truths would rip the webbing that holds
the world in place. I'll never teach *The Golden Bowl*—even grad students might insist on finding
a single culprit, or demand an outburst, somewhere in those labyrinthine paragraphs,
of uncorseted, unchaperoned emotion. Despite my awkward gluing job, the fluted edges
of that vase lifted for all those years like petals, satiny as the hems fluttering around
Grandma's nylon-stockinged legs that tottered under the weight of far too many whiskeys
while she held my hand, stroked my hair, and called me precious. Melting together various colors
of glass causes the opalescence of favrile. There's an exercise I like to give in writing
workshops: Imagine you're holding an heirloom vase in your hands. Turn it around, feel its shape,
its smooth or grainy, pebbly texture. Now look down into it, where at the bottom you'll see
a wisp of thread or a hairline crack. Which is it? What happens next? Maybe in time
one student will find a tattered copy of the book, will open it with a careful hand, so
the pages won't crumble, the spine doesn't break.

Wang Wei in the Workshop

Twelve hundred years
since the eighth century.
Of nineteen translations,
we've looked at five.
Lily is crying after
reading her poem
about her home city
of Hong Kong, where,
in a building designed
for ten dozen stories,
six men hauling waste
died when the elevator
shaft collapsed and
plunged twenty floors.
From that roof, no one
sees the house
of a small family
eating from porcelain
bowls on a wooden
table balanced
on level ground.
How can a moon
slip so far down
those concrete walls?

Langston Hughes' "Weary Blues"

Needs no explaining in this class. No one needs a gloss
on "Suicide's Note," that river so calm, asking a kiss,
yet none of us around this table
has ever been kept out of a KFC or a multiplex
because of our skin. "Nobody knows the trouble
I've seen," sang Lena Horne, who couldn't stay
at the Savoy-Plaza after she'd
made the crowd swing. Enough trouble right here
in this room. Ann's just driven from the hospice,
her gay dad's body shriveling into the sheets,
her mother and brothers refusing
to visit. Last week Robert's cousins were found
mangled by the train tracks in Sabinas for the Los Zetas
dope they were running, only way to pay for beans
and rice. This morning in my office
Christina soaked through the six tissues I offered
as she told how the fucked-up ex-marine raped her
in the ass over and over, his loaded .45 beside
the pillow. No wonder Hughes'
pianist "stopped playing and went to bed," where
he "slept like a rock or a man that's dead." I need
to focus on the poem, call and response, structure
of the blues. Nathan might help,
he's a musician. But already he's talking: "Hey, after
class, how many of y'all want to drive over to JJ's, awesome
piano, sax, bass." And all I say is, "Count me in."

Why I Dread Teaching *The Sun Also Rises*

When I used to picture the whole class, all fifty-six of us, lounging
around a bar, sprawled under a fly-ridden
fan creaking overhead with a bartender listening like a burnt-out priest
and a throaty half-lidded alto crooning to a mike,
I'd forget that always, even after I deliver my riff about World War One
and life in the trenches where the guys
watched their buddies' brains explode into bloody pulp after wading
for months in mud up to their knees,
one of the students, maybe Tiffany, will begin to whine, "This book
is disgusting, why should we care about no-good
drunks wandering around destroying their God-given bodies,
and as for Brett, she's a total slut, the fact
that Jake loves her tells you how sick he is, and anyway, why do we
have to read such depressing novels?"
Then Bryan will say, "Yeah, she's right, and how come these dudes
can afford to eat in all these pricey restaurants,"
and even after William chimes in to counter that Jake actually has a job,
Bryan will sneer, "Sure, he works maybe five minutes
between drinks"—and it's uphill work to steer the class back on track,
ask them if they've ever been hurt so badly
all they want to do is forget, but if I'm lucky it'll be William who pipes up
again to say, "Haven't y'all done Fiesta, come on,
you know how you party nonstop till you find out which of your friends
are the real jerks, the serious assholes, and
then you know the score, aren't fooled by anybody any more." Maybe
I used to remember the year when I traveled
with a cousin and his group of musicians, summer afternoons in Verona
over a three-hour lunch before the concert
when the notes of Vivaldi flew to the dome of the cathedral and lived
in my ears all the next day and the next as we ordered
Campari and soda before the evening's *passegiatta*, the long lounging
at a round table as we watched the women and men
saunter and the *ragazzi* jostle and the swallows lift above the piazza,
swirl and dip while the sun dropped and the sky

turned rose, before a few of us found a little *ristorante* and ordered trout
caught that morning from a stream in the Dolomites
where later we walked in meadows so far above the cars and smoke
we thought we'd been lofted to a snow-glazed heaven.
During those months I forgot everything but the sweet tang of the air.
But that's not the whole of it, not really the truth.
How I worked to forget the nights when that cousin was so drunk
he made Mike in the novel look like a hero,
made Frances' sniping at Robert Cohn look sweet and kind, the way
he'd yell at his girlfriend and call her "bitch,"
the way his hands would slide over the breasts and bottoms of women
before they even realized he'd crossed that boundary
right out in public, and why nobody slugged him I still don't know.
But then there was the semester when Guadalupe
perked up the class by saying that the novel reminded her of childhood
in Monterrey, when her father took the family
to the Plaza de Toros on Sundays and explained why the *torero* wears
a suit of lights decorated with gold and silver threads,
and how he uses the long skinny sword only for killing, how it's all a ritual,
and that—just like Jake tells Brett—you're supposed
to focus on the bull, on every little movement, so it's not so horrible,
it's like a ballet, a dance, though with death, and
so graceful it's kind of beautiful, but even so, she found it hard to see
all the blood, and hardest to watch the horses.
The students were lined up in rows of unmoveable desks, and
one of the fluorescent bulbs overhead
flickered on and off as the room grew quiet and nobody rustled a page.
It's not so easy to spot grace under pressure.
I always wanted to be one of the insiders—not a whiner,
sentimental, squeamish, like Robert Cohn.
When I taught *Lord of the Flies* to high school seniors, a couple of boys
brought in a bloody pig's head dripping
in a paper bag, and I only said, "Cool, where did you guys get that?"
These days I can't stomach anything stronger
than San Pellegrino after years as a Johnny Walker on the rocks

wannabe aficionado, and I've never been in a war.
But I know how it feels when someone in a group, even in a family,
goes berserk like a maddened bull, how it feels when
from out of nowhere, talk fired like a mortar shell explodes the head
sitting next to you, maybe your own, open
down to the bone, with no one who can bring together the viscous
edges of the wound, and you're so numb
all you can do is try to walk without stumbling, focus on the next step,
the next drink, even if it's orange juice, because
this bull won't give up the ghost with a straight swoop of a blade.
What you want is to go off alone and dive
into deep, clean water, start over with no carnage anywhere in sight,
as if you could, and isn't it pretty to think so.

Whenever We've Dipped into *Walden*

Some sophomore will say "Sure, okay, I get Thoreau's
whole 'tonic of wildness' thing, but it's not so noble
to live off by yourself with the beavers,"
and I'll almost agree, till I remember sailing through
Norwegian fjords with a hankering to live out my days
gazing at larches and spruce, whirling
gulls and waterfalls. Those inlets more pristine than
Squam, the New Hampshire lake where I splashed
in the shallows before I could walk. But
living alone on a sub-arctic slope, I'd shrivel to a brittle
husk. Not only Squam's dappling birch leaves, expanse
of water beyond the pine needles
clustered in bundles snug as my sisters and me tucked in
our cots—we had those silvery nights and days together,
no alarms jangling us awake and
shoving us off to separate schools in buses crammed with
jostling kids. We didn't know then how often Grandpop
bellowed at Daddy after breakfast
or that Grandma drank herself dizzy before dinner,
didn't know why Mom ignored speed limits careening
into Plymouth for aspirin and
more sherry. Nightmares never infected our sleep
in the cottage where ancestors had dressed to be married,
no naggings interrupted our Nestlé's
cocoa in the high-raftered hall beside the field where our
great-uncles' horseshoes clanked before Vespers. Invisible,
our dead, like rings inside the white
pines. My sisters and I bestowed secret names on every
granite boulder we climbed. But over the years we drifted,
driven by calendars and deadlines,
by fears of Mom's sporadic rages, Daddy's withdrawals, hissed
breaths, the jangling ice in his highballs. And our jealousies:
which of us was prettiest, smartest,

nicest, which one Mom prized most. "We do not treat ourselves
nor one another thus tenderly," said Thoreau. Yet now after
funerals and weddings, divorces,
remarriages, after a son-in-law's suicide, a brother's multiple
myeloma, we've returned to the lake. During class, one
student will always remind us
that Henry David didn't exactly make it on his own
while squatting on Emerson's land, since friends stopped by
to talk about books, his mother
brought him fresh-baked blueberry pies, and he'd stroll
into the village for gossip and cornmeal. How could I
"suck out all the marrow of life"
if I were alone? By that New Hampshire lake, the past rests
underfoot like pine needles softening to silt. Last June,
after the semester's end, when my sisters
and I returned to Squam, while they were off with husbands
and kids, canoeing or napping on the porch or finishing
another 3000-piece puzzle, a familial quiet
pillowed the granite stone I leaned on, formed from the earth's
magma how many eons ago, those volcanic eruptions
that solidified into the rockbed
holding me to one small ridge, one ripple in a vast open
bowl, the lake where water is always leaving to become air.

Preparing Jeffers' "Vulture" Before Class

I'm already predicting the reaction: "Who cares 'how beautiful
he looked,' that bird gliding 'on those great sails,'
this guy is freaking weird
if he wants to be shredded like that." So I'm wondering if I should
mention what happened a year ago when
I turned from a booth on
wind power at our neighborhood's GreenFest to face a Eurasian
Eagle Owl on a man's gloved arm. Stared right
into me. I don't know
how long I froze, swept into that centered gaze. I guess tonight
I could propose that maybe death Jeffers' way
wouldn't be worse than
the doctors' slipping a gastric feeding tube into my father's
stomach, puncturing his lung, then jamming
a ventilating tube down
his throat, after which he never talked again. "Iatrogenic mishaps,"
such things are called, the complications, side
effects of common medical
procedures, like the euphemism "therapies" for the chiseling
through bone, the screws in my mother's knees,
the implanted defibrillator
that shocked her heart back to its familiar thud after it had
wrenched to a stop. Finally she gave up eating,
and then, even water. She'd
never read the Dylan Thomas poem, never raged against
the dying of the light. I know what Goethe
said, but is it really light
that leaves? I've read accounts of mystics who talk of luminosity,
radiance that beckons, leads them to die in
utter calm. That Eagle Owl,
its clean ferocity—a moment nothing short of rapture. No wonder
people say those birds connect us with
the universe. As if to scoff

at all our needles, tubes, the tinkerings, machinery we submit to,
hoping we'll delay what has to come. But
the vulture, Jeffers knew,
feeds only on flesh no longer living, and, even then, a social
bird, it calls to neighboring flocks to join
in cleaning up the land,
this bird that, for the Pueblo people, signaled purification. The Parsi
Zoroastrians exposed their dead on "towers
of silence," a final act
of charity, providing the birds with food that otherwise would
go to waste. *Cathartes Aura*: "Golden
Purifier"—in Buddhism,
compassion. Which is spacious, patient, allowing for existing
things to change. I remember reading
that once a toddler was
found on a mountain peak beside a vulture. He'd been missing
for three days, but was smiling, utterly
unhurt, though on his
grimy shirt were pierced two sets of talon marks, a rip
from a hooked beak. "What an
enskyment," says
Jeffers. What a way to begin a life, or, I'm thinking, end.

Innisfree, They Get

These sophomores understand a lake—or the South
Texas shore, the Gulf. But they don't
know the birds. Or plants, or flowers. Today
with Williams' poem, Queen Anne's lace has never
been so remote a thing, and though
just north of town it takes the fields by force,
these kids have never noticed. I draw
an image on the board: the umbel
and its dozens of florets. My art work's
lame, but now the flower's in focus. I say
I know they've seen the grasses along
the interstate, the way in a breeze they dip
and sway, and just imagine a whole field
of these white blossoms trembling
like a single body that quivers from simply
being touched. Last month when reading
Yeats, everyone knew that primal
longing for water, if not an Irish lake,
then the pond at an opa's hill country ranch,
or the creek by an abuelo's house
near the border. Some even knew
that Yeats' bean rows referred to *Walden*,
and each one of them, I could tell
from their eyes, wanted peace to come
dropping slow. Laptops sat inert beside
that vision. But even I hadn't known
that Yeats' linnet was not some uniquely
Irish avian creature, but close cousin
to the same red house finch that flocks
to my own feeder, perches in our live oaks
and pittosporum every day, in the deep
core of my own life, where—and this
I won't tell the students—you are with me,
day and night, the fibers of that touch,
all a glimmer, and right here, at home.

I'm Not Sure the Cherry Is the "Loveliest of Trees"

So from the first line of the poem I'm quibbling,
and I don't even teach this poem now
I'm pushing threescore and ten. All that counting
Housman has us busy doing, figuring
the speaker's age, and I know in class we'd end up
focusing on the stanzas with the math. Yet
students never had trouble getting hold
of the poem's carpe diem message: inhale
the scent of roses while you can. I've never seen
a flowering cherry, have never known
spring in Washington D.C. or England or
been invited to a *hanami*, a party to view
the blooms in Tokyo. But I knew the dogwoods
lacing my first hesitant steps, have known
white pines' needles gleaming with
light reflected from a northern lake, and
I've known the palo verdes in the dusty Sonoran
desert where Rudy, my first boyfriend,
kissed me. And the olives I planted
with my former husband, shoveling down
into Phoenix hardpan. The eucalyptus lifting
their astringent scent in the Berkeley hills
where I lay in a carpet of fog-softened leaves, ecstatic
with a lover. The lemon tree by the front door
of the house where my son was born. I could say
"with rue my heart is laden" for these and all
the trees I may never see again: banyans and teak,
neem trees, cinnamon and coconut palms,
the bodhi tree—under which the Buddha
sat so still. And since I haven't many springs
left in me—a dozen? two?—maybe,
like the woman diagnosed with terminal
cancer who traveled seven continents
compiling a life list of eight thousand birds,

I could search out all the trees I've never seen,
including the blossoming cherry. In California
there's a bristlecone that's lived for almost
five thousand years, and in Sweden, a spruce
that's lived for close to ten. That woman's travels
kept her cancer in remission, her doctors
were amazed. But how can I leave our own
Mexican persimmon near the drive, its peeling
layers of coppery silver bark, its branching
trunk I can't begin to wrap my arms around?

Coming to Cather

I'm still afloat from last night's performance of Mahler's Fourth,
and the room is strangely silent till Michele
looks up and whispers,
"This is the best book of the semester." Everyone nods, but
their eyes are vague, unfocused, as if they're
surrounded by an earthen
sea of gramas and bluestems, wading through prairie
grasses that once stretched from Manitoba
down into Cather's Nebraska
and on into Texas. It's time to get the class going, but I can't
block out that theme from the third movement,
the violins. A relief
when Charlotte speaks up, says her family came from the same
Bohemia as Ántonia's, and that her great-grandfather
built violins, violas, and
cellos for his wife and kids, their own double string
quartet. She insists, "He'd never have committed
suicide like Ántonia's dad." But
Jason says, "It could zap anybody's spirit, plowing unbroken
sod," and Geoffrey adds that "Ántonia's father
was a really talented
musician, respected in the old country, so how could he
be a farmer, no surprise he shot himself, living
in a dugout hovel." I hear
the strings again, the violinists' bows lifting at the same
moment like the grasses in a breeze, stems
bending in one
direction. But I bring myself back to the book, and
we linger over lines describing the prairie grass
that "was the country,
as the water is the sea." Years ago, moving to Texas, I felt
adrift as if I'd entered Cather's novel, living
as we did on a parcel of land

out of town, no neighbors in sight. I tell the class about
the Polish word *tęsknota*: stronger than our
"nostalgia," meaning "pain
of distance." The sound of those cellos in the Mahler. My then
husband tried to grow all our own food. Wanted
goats, chickens, melons,
corn. Acres of land we couldn't afford, bugs, rabbits, deer,
hot wind biting at the garden, bad weather chewing
on the marriage. The dogs'
tails whisked through waves of the grasses like fins. How
that husband filled our narrow house with music,
sounds of his viola, silky
tenor lofting toward the trees. No human voice in Mahler's
Fourth till the last movement. A lone soprano
singing of a childlike heaven. It was
a long drive into town those years, as we tried to keep the pair of
ourselves afloat. Only five minutes left in the class
and I need to wrap things up,
explain next week's assignment. But I wish all twenty-two of us
could pile into our cars, caravan out to the hills
where now in November
the grasses are seeding. Mahler's work begins and ends
in a different key. I haven't wanted to return
to the place where the marriage
went under. Twelve, maybe fifteen years have passed
and finally, I hear the symphony, whole again.

The Morning After Our Second Ecopoetry Class

I'm online reading that our infant universe rang
with reverberations of cosmic bells that rippled the primordial
darkness like a pond pounded by stones, and I'm still
thinking about Daniel's puzzlement last night
over the essay "Nature and Silence," in which Christopher Manes
argues we need to listen to the language of the world
beyond our human words. But even though Melanie
brought drawings showing how the Chinese ideogram for *bird*
developed from an image of an actual bird, and even
though I explained that *aleph* and the letter *A*
came from the Phoenician symbol for ox, Daniel was not alone
in wondering how rocks could speak. We talked
for half an hour about the way words can mask,
serve as distractions. Once, at Tortuguero, about to go zip-lining,
six of us chattered away on the platform a hundred
and fifty feet above the rain forest floor until
we let loose to zoom along the cable over the canopy, the kids
whooping like howlers, those raucous monkeys whose
cries I'd mistaken for rowdies at the hotel bar
the night before. We sped over trees so fast we couldn't have
seen a motmot or aracari if it had flitted right below
our ankles. On the ground, our guide pointed out
Jesus Christ lizards and spectacled caimans I might have mistaken
for logs. He knew the calls of manakins, oropendolas,
and toucans—he would stop and cock his head
to listen—but oh, how he would natter. Kayaking in the midst
of mangroves thick with the absence of human prattle,
he'd be rapid-firing details about the next
day's agenda. One midnight, four of us followed a local guy
onto the beach, the tide thrumming its mantra
beneath a spangling of stars. It wasn't long
before the green sea turtles dragged their four-hundred-pound
bodies onto the beach to dig their nests. We stood

beside one as she dropped a hundred eggs down
into the hollowed sand. Other than the rustle of surf, there was
no sound but the dry chuff, sigh, the gasp she gave
between each batch of half a dozen glistening eggs,
the flesh within the carapace gathering strength for the next
long push. These creatures have been around
for two hundred million years. Hindus say
it's a giant turtle that holds up the world. Next Thursday
I'll tell the class about that night, how none of us spoke,
even walking back up the beach and
down the road. But how to describe a silence that echoes
in the rocky crust, the mantle of my bones.

Teaching "The Red Wheelbarrow" the 30th Time

I know I've explained how
Williams didn't like tapping
tired old symbols, but
these sophomores are
not convinced. They've
got that wheelbarrow hard
at work: it symbolizes life, since
it's red, like blood; they've
got it carrying feed, back and
forth from the coop to keep
those chickens alive so
they can be busy laying eggs,
though they're white, which
stands for death. Susanna
says the poem is about
her grandpa, up at four
and out to the barn. I'm tired
of chatter, of words dragged
around to mean what they
don't. I'm tired of stories,
of somebody always *doing* something, or not
doing what somebody
wishes they would. Tired of the whole
subject-verb-object paradigm. I'd
even like erasing
the prepositions in the poem,
deleting "beside" and "with." I want
only the barrow, feathers, and
water left from rain. Separate,
not even in relation, as
with the elements of a T'ang Dynasty poem,
the kind Williams loved,
the sort he and
Rexroth translated. Just
the Chinese characters

like drawings, the blank
spaces breaths, each one
itself: wheelbarrow, red, rain water, chickens,
white. There's
a quiet I want that won't happen
in this discussion,
a silence that comes after
long rain, the hush
when you swear you can
feel the swirl of
planets, the shifting
of rocks. I should lead
the class outside; we could
sit on the grass, look
at a red bud
tree, an empty
stone bench. But somehow
I end up telling a story
after all, the one about
Williams the doctor
having just explained to a mother and father
their child would die, or
was it the child
had died and
he had to break the news. Then
he walked down
the hall and stared out the window
at a wheelbarrow and a few
chickens. Now
the whole class is with me. I don't
remember where
I heard the story. I'm not sure
it's even true. The poem itself is
silent. You can't hear
any clucking.

After Spring Break, Arriving at Pound's "In a Station of the Metro"

I'm just home from five days of slogging through overcoats and umbrellas and feet, cold
pavement in New York. Weary of crowds. "How can this be a poem?" asks Jay, and—
though for years I've loved these two lines—I hesitate, thinking: if Pound's "Petals on a wet,
black bough" are like faces in a crowd, they must be wilted, bruised by the hammering
clamor of hustle and need. "It's about ghosts," Jennifer insists, "or at least dead people, and
someone's putting flowers by a grave. The bough," she goes on, "is the casket, and the crowd's
the family, everybody's crying, so the bough's wet with tears." But Graciela says she knows
they call the subway system in Paris "Le Métro," so the poem is "a metaphor showing
how people in the dirty underground tunnel look fresh, like flowers." Thirty heads lift and nod,
and for a split second I'm back in line at La Guardia's Gate B5 waiting to buy a bottle of water,
my carry-on slicing into my shoulder, as the faces around me swivel like sunflowers
toward the sun when a teenage boy whispers, "It's her, *it is*, it's Halle Berry," and suddenly we're all
abloom, a petaled row leading to one specimen rose, even as our feet cramp
into the tile floor. "I get it," says Molly. "This is about the surreal feeling you'd have
in a subway, a rush of people, and you don't know anyone. Still, you feel every human being
is delicate." I tell them that the poem grew after Pound was stunned by the flood
of faces emerging from the Métro at La Concorde, how he struggled to compress

thirty lines into twenty seed-packed words. Molly's
right that we're ephemeral as
flowers, and Jennifer may not be so far off after all,
for none of us—not Halle Berry, not
this classroom, nothing, except perhaps the subway
tracks and colonies of rats,
and possibly, improbably, Pound's poem—will last.

Arriving at Wallace Stevens in the 13th Week

I borrow an apple from Amy, place it on the carpet, and ask
what's changed, as we stare at this red and yellow
freckled luminescence, our circled desks surrounding the mind
of nothing in our midst, altered by the various
blues of our various guitars. We agree "Study of Two Pears"
is about pears, but "The Idea of Order at Key West"
hums beyond the genius of these walls, and twenty pairs of eyes
puzzle over wide-open Nortons till Tony proclaims
the singer in the poem to be the moon, since it's always pulling
at the tides, causing the ocean's roar. But
tonight I stifle my irritation that he's found what isn't there
in the poem's portrayal of a woman's seaside
singing. For once I let Tony be artificer of his own notes,
even if dimly starred, as he strides alongside
the poem, thwarting my blessed rage for order honed by forty
years in classrooms. Yet I want him to slip
barefoot into the poem's curling surf, want him to swim out
into the noctilucent swell of it with no guiding moon
or pinpoint of harbor light, just the rise and fall of the waves
with their unpredictable lines, the undertow
of the water's elastic weight, though I don't want him to drown,
and maybe I'm the one who's deaf to songs
along the shore, to hymns that buzz beside my ears. Maybe
I can follow only one blackbird at a time,
blind to the undulate spangles of another's sense of things.

Next-to-Last Week in the Senior Workshop

We're all chuckling over Brad's anti-football
poem, and awed by Meg's poem
on puberty rites among the Diegueño
of Baja, California, and, while everyone's
tuckered by this time in the semester, there's
a warmth in the room that wasn't here
in September or even October when the temps
hovered in the nineties, a comfort sewn
by fourteen minds bent over each other's
poems so that week by week we've all
knitted into each other, and now,
when it's time to end, it feels like layers
of skin being peeled. Sometimes, even
the best students won't bother to find me
in my office after winter break to retrieve
their portfolios. Most I'll never see
after finals. How I want to hang on, as if they're
my own children, say, "Keep in touch,"
"Don't get lost." And though after each
semester ends, it feels like sailing out
into open seas, unencumbered space,
fresh winds, I always fear it may be
me I'm losing, as if, without those voices
every week, I won't know what game
I'm playing, won't know what rituals
to follow, as if I won't find land again.

Books, Bath Towels, and Beyond

After Gary asked, "Will we ever read
any normal people in this class?" and I quipped,
"No, of course not," and after the laughter had quieted,
we ambled through "Song of Myself," celebrating
our "respiration and inspiration," traveling along
with the voices of sailors, prostitutes, presidents, and tree-toads,
in sync with the poet's vision. No one
this time—not even Gary—grumbled about
Whitman's disgusting ego, and yet when we came to the place
where God is "a loving bedfellow"
who leaves "baskets covered with white towels
bulging the house with their plenty," I was the one who
wanted to stop. At that point, I've always
been puzzled. I get it that a lover could
be like a god. But *towels*? We'd just finished *The House
of the Seven Gables*, and I wondered if
Hepzibah or Phoebe ever sold linens in their shop. Yet
we never hear Hawthorne talking about blankets or sheets or
how anybody washes his face or her hands,
let alone armpits or "soft-tickling genitals"—leave
those to Uncle Walt. The store Hepzibah opened: a first step
in easing the grip of her cursed
ancestors, of joining the sunlit world. Last summer
when my husband and I moved back into our old house after
a massive redo, we gave away box after box
of sweaters and tchotchkes. We even disposed of old
books, including those with my neon markings in the margins
blunt as Gary's outbursts in class: "Ugh,"
"NO," and "Wow!" It was time to loosen the mind
beyond the nub of the old self. My mother used to huff through
the house every year like a great wind,
and when she settled down, not a doll over
twelve months old remained, not a dress, not a scarf, not even

lint wisping in a drawer. One year during
a flood, my husband's letters from lifelong friends
drowned in the garage, morphed back into pulp. I never hoped
the past would vanish into a blank, and yet,
when Holgrave in the novel cries, "Shall we never,
never get rid of this Past?" I, too, want it washed clean, to wake
in the morning released from echoes
of my father's muttered invectives, my mother's
searing tongue. I've now torn to rags the rust-stained towels
from my former marriage and
my husband's bachelorhood sheets, raveled
threads drooping like fishnets. How Hawthorne's Phoebe
opened that heavy-lidded house
to the light. I used to scorn her chirpy domesticity,
praying along with Emily Dickinson—whose balance
Gary had also questioned—"God keep me
from what they call *households*." And yet, after
my husband and I returned to our remade, renewed house,
what did I do but go shopping
for towels. Back and forth to seven strip malls,
bringing home only to return I don't know how many colors,
till finally, I settled on white. And as I
pulled out my MasterCard to pay for the contents
of my brimming cart, a gaunt, wizened man entered
the check-out line, hands pressing
to his chest two white towels just like mine,
eyes lifted to the ceiling as if in prayer. I doubt that Gary
would think it normal to greet the divine
while clutching terry cloth. But now I see
that Whitman knew what fresh towels could mean for a dazed
and puffy face, white towels unspecked by blood
or errant coils of hair, towels that spill from a basket
like sea-foam. Like cirrus clouds adrift while we're loafing
on tender, newly sprouted blades of grass
growing from the loam under our boot soles,
from graves of the old and decaying, all we've finally buried.

In Our Class on Roethke

Jennifer's complaining he's really a wimp,
his endings don't grab her. "And what's more,
in 'The Waking,' he sounds drugged,
like maybe he's dying," says Jennifer, adding
she feels the poem is about death, since
it made her depressed, especially "that worm
climbing the winding stair." I almost holler out
she's got it wrong, that's not the poem I've loved.
But who can tell how light will take a tree,
predict the progressions of shadow shifting
into sun. We've just slipped back
into our chairs, after a trek across campus
to watch Tibetan monks tip grains of sand
around edges of the mandala that tomorrow
they'll efface, an illustration of Wallace Stevens'
mantra we've discussed, the only constant is change.
I'm grateful for Daniel, who says the poem
is about what the monks are doing, filling in
that space, grain of sand by grain of sand,
taking it slow. "And then, it'll all be gone," says Daniel,
adding, "It's hard to imagine
investing so much in something that won't last."
A measured way, the monks' design.
And one I've tried to learn to practice, studying
to forget the frantic hurry-skurry memorized
at my mother's knee. The last word she ever spoke
was "quick," and "quick" again, as if the dance
could never end too soon. Great Nature always
has that other thing to do to us—but
now I guess I must explain how Roethke
suffered from despair, yet how he also
learned to sing and whistle, romping with the bears
along the living ground. I say aloud,

"This poem is one I'd like someone to read
if there's a funeral when I die," and
Brittany says, "Oh please don't even think that way."
These students here beside me, every
Thursday evening, all semester. A week
till finals, then it's over. Our syllables
commingling, little speech-threaders. They keep
my shaking steady. Line by phrase,
word by breath, we learn by going, as we go.

Ending the Semester in American Lit

The guy who served as a lighthouse
when discussions had grown so foggy I couldn't
steer us back on course—the one who never missed
a class, who camped in my office every
Wednesday afternoon obsessed with Bartleby
and Ahab, made all A's and wrote a dynamite final—
hasn't turned in his long essay. Is he
bleeding on a gurney in the ER, or moaning
by the freeway in a pile of smashed glass and mangled
chrome? I email, and he shoots back, "I haven't
written it." No apology, no excuse. I offer an
extra day. No response, not even to say he prefers
not to. I want to harpoon that essay and
splatter it onto my desk. I give him till
midnight, remind him, bold font on the syllabus:
"No essay, no passing grade." Still silence,
nada, no paper. Where *is* that essay? I feel
like Herman's wife Lizzie, nagging him, or Carlyle,
insisting, "Produce! Produce!" Melville's
narrator at least learned about his clerk's past
at the dead letter office, but I have no idea where
this guy works, or if he does. Is he playing
some kind of game, resisting like Bartleby,
forcing me to play Ahab, hunt him down? Why
can't I just give him an F? I've become
the narrator in Melville's story, his whole career
questioned by the scrivener's refusals. Maybe I'm
remembering my years as a grad student
when I skimped time with my son to write
all those essays, the dread dissertation, and, then, later,
meet deadlines for grades, committee
reports. Updating the CV to show every
minuscule pebble I cast into the scholarly sea. All those

sleepy post-Christmas days I missed—leaving
my boy and his dad in their jammies—to join
the tangled academic throngs at the MLA. On this guy's
final exam he added a note that said
our class had changed him, he'd been on course
to become like Ahab, netting every A in sight, but after
finishing *Moby-Dick* and then reading
Whitman, he decided to spend more time with
his daughter, who's just learning to walk, and he didn't
want to miss a single one of her
wobbling steps, he felt the pull to "loafe
and invite" his soul. But I'm left here anchorless,
like Melville's ship the *Rachel*
searching after her missing sailors, her lost children.

The Last Time I Taught Robert Frost

I shuddered when Olivia, who is writing her dissertation
on dialectics of the self in Gloria Anzaldúa, announced she found him
lovely. "Lovely?" I cried, professional composure shot,
my image of Frost collapsing suddenly as the Great Stone Face
on Cannon Mountain, the craggy Old Man fallen in shards
to the ground. True, this was not on par with the vandalizing
of his house in Vermont, Homer Noble Farm's wicker chairs,
wooden tables, dressers smashed and thrown into the fire to keep
the place warm while thirty kids swilled a hundred and fifty
cans of Bud with a dozen bottles of Jack Daniel's, and threw up
on the floor. After all, Olivia wasn't saying she didn't like
the poems, but *lovely*? A word my mother detested as phony,
like someone holding a pinkie straight out while drinking tea,
the sort of word my grandmother used when vaguely praising
a Bartók piece, or a play she didn't understand. Like people
saying, "How interesting," when what they really mean is, "Spare me
the details," or, "Could we change the subject." So when
I asked Olivia what she meant by "lovely" and she talked about
the lush, long vowel sounds, I wondered why I'd felt stabbed,
until I remembered my father's lying in the ICU, the fat respirator
tube jammed down his throat, the whoosh of forced breath
fogging the glassed-in-room, and my stroking his forehead while
my father, whom I'd never seen cry, began to leak tears down
his chiseled face. Finally, not knowing what more to do, I stood
by the window staring out at the New Hampshire pines
and began reciting one of his favorite poems: "I must go down
to the seas again, to the lonely sea and the sky." He started
to jerk, whole body spasms under the sheets, more tears carving
runnels down his cheeks, and I knew he wanted me to recite
"Stopping By Woods," his most-loved poem and maybe mine too,
but I couldn't. I couldn't turn from that window looking
out at the trees beyond the parking lot, the words to the one
poem I've known by heart for decades buried somewhere
below my throat. He died the next day. Maybe that was why
I asked the class if we could recite it, if perhaps some of them

even had it memorized, and Denise and Lupe and Nathaniel actually said they had. So we chanted it, the other eight of us

reading from the Norton's crisp, white pages, but when we came to the ending, not a single student needed to look down

as we sang the last stanza all together. I can't explain it, but for once something dark and deep entered among us in the overly

air-conditioned room. As if we were all one self and yet still alone in the cold, and wanting to stay. When we spoke again,

we talked until I had to stand up, open the door, and tell them to leave, say it was past time for their dinners and

all the lovely, nagging promises waiting for them to keep.

Wendy Barker's novel in prose poems, *Nothing Between Us: The Berkeley Years* (runner-up for the Del Sol Prize) was released by Del Sol Press in 2009. Earlier full-length collections of poetry include *Poems from Paradise* (WordTech, 2005), *Way of Whiteness* (Wings Press, 2000), *Let the Ice Speak* (Ithaca House, 1991), and *Winter Chickens* (Corona Publishing, 1990). Wendy has also published four chapbooks, *From the Moon, Earth Is Blue* (Wings Press, 2015), *Things of the Weather* (Pudding House Press, 2009), *Between Frames* (Pecan Grove Press, 2006) and *Eve Remembers* (Aark Arts, 1996).

A selection of poems accompanied by autobiographical essays, *Poems' Progress* (Absey & Co.), appeared in 2002, and a collection of translations (with Saranindranath Tagore) from the Bengali of India's Nobel Prize-winning poet, *Rabindranath Tagore: Final Poems* (George Braziller, 2001), received the Sourette Diehl Fraser Award from the Texas Institute of Letters.

Wendy's poems and translations have appeared in many journals, including *Poetry*, *Southern Review*, *Georgia Review*, *Gettysburg Review*, *The American Scholar*, *Kenyon Review*, *New Letters*, *Nimrod*, *Stand*, *Partisan Review*, *Michigan Quarterly Review*, *Antioch*, and *Southern Poetry Review*. Her work has also been included in numerous anthologies, including *The Best American Poetry 2013* (eds. Denise Duhamel and David Lehman). Essays have appeared in such magazines as *Poets & Writers* and *Southwest Review*.

She has read her poetry at dozens of universities, bookstores, festivals, and conferences in the United States, Europe, and in India. As a scholar, she is the author of *Lunacy of Light: Emily Dickinson and the Experience of Metaphor* (Southern Illinois University Press, 1987) as well as co-editor (with Sandra M. Gilbert) of *The House Is Made of Poetry: The Art of Ruth Stone* (Southern Illinois University Press, 1996).

Recipient of an NEA fellowship, a Rockefeller residency fellowship at Bellagio, as well as other awards in poetry, including the Writers' League of Texas Book Award (which she has received twice, for *Way of Whiteness* in 2000 and for *Between Frames* in 2007) and the Mary Elinore Smith Poetry Prize from *The American Scholar*, she has also been a Fulbright senior lecturer in Bulgaria. Her work has been translated into Hindi, Chinese, Japanese, Russian, and Bulgarian.

She is poet-in-residence and the Pearl LeWinn professor of creative writing at the University of Texas at San Antonio, where she has taught since 1982. Wendy has one son, David Barker, and is married to the critic and biographer Steven G. Kellman.

Winners of the John Ciardi Prize for Poetry:

The Resurrection Machine by Steve Gehrke, selected by Miller Williams

Kentucky Swami by Tim Skeen, selected by Michael Burns

Escape Artist by Terry Blackhawk, selected by Molly Peacock

Fence Line by Curtis Bauer, selected by Christopher Buckley

The Portable Famine by Rane Arroyo, selected by Robin Becker

Wayne's College of Beauty by David Swanger, selected by Colleen J. McElroy

Airs & Voices by Paula Bonnell, selected by Mark Jarman

Black Tupelo Country by Doug Ramspeck, selected by Leslie Adrienne Miller

Tongue of War by Tony Barnstone, selected by B. H. Fairchild

Mapmaking by Megan Harlan, selected by Sidney Wade

Secret Wounds by Richard M. Berlin, selected by Gary Young

Axis Mundi by Karen Holmberg, selected by Lorna Dee Cervantes

Beauty Mark by Suzanne Cleary, selected by Kevin Prufer

Border States by Jane Hoogestraat, selected by Luis J. Rodríguez

One Blackbird at a Time by Wendy Barker, selected by Alice Friman